D1830839

# USEFUL
# SANSKRIT NOUNS AND VERBS
## IN ENGLISH LETTERS

Owing to the antiquity and rarity of this book, certain pages are regrettably absent, and readability is compromised due to the blurring of the original text. If you possess any insights regarding the availability of these missing sections, kindly inform us. Your assistance is crucial in ensuring the completion of this significant work for the benefit of future generations.

# USEFUL SANSKRIT NOUNS AND VERBS

## IN ENGLISH LETTERS

COMPILER

**CHARLES JOHNSTON**

GYAN

*Published by*

GYAN

Gyan Publishing House
5, Ansari Road
Daryaganj, New Delhi-110002
Phone: 011-47034999, 9811692060
E-mail: books@gyanbooks.com

*Distribution Network*
gyanbooks.com
India, USA, Canada, UK, Australia

**© Publisher**

All rights reserved. No part of this work may be reproduced, stored, adapted, or transmitted in any form or by any means, electronic, mechanical, photocopying, micro-filming, recording or otherwise, or translated in any language, without the prior written permission of the copyright owner and the publisher.

ISBN: 978-93-6920-045-0 (HB)

First Published, 1892

2nd Impression 2025

*Printed at:* Gyan Press, Delhi.

The book is sold subject to the condition that it shall not, by way of trade or otherwise, be lent, resold, hired out, or otherwise circulated without the prior publisher's written consent.

**USEFUL SANSKRIT NOUNS AND VERBS**
Compiler: CHARLES JOHNSTON

# USEFUL

# SANSKRIT NOUNS AND VERBS.

*IN ENGLISH LETTERS.*

COMPILED BY

CHARLES JOHNSTON,

BENGAL CIVIL SERVICE; DUBLIN UNIVERSITY SANSKRIT PRIZEMAN;
INDIA CIVIL SERVICE SANSKRIT PRIZEMAN.

"*Nocturnâ versate manu, versate diurnâ.*"

LONDON: LUZAC & CO.

1892.

# PREFACE.

NEED I say that this little book does not claim to be more than an introduction to Sanskrit grammar? It owes its existence to the practical difficulty which I have felt in putting before students the simple declensions and conjugations in a form in which they might most easily be learnt by heart.

The grammars of Professors Max-Müller, Whitney, and Sir M. Monier-Williams are open to the objection that beginners are compelled to pick out the transliterated forms from amongst the Devanâgarî, while advanced students are under the opposite difficulty: their attention, following the line of least resistance, is led away from the Devanâgarî forms to the English letters, and thus important differences are overlooked.

The ideal grammar would contain these two elements separated: first, a section containing the rules, and all forms transliterated, and then the Devanâgarî forms printed separately, so that the eye might follow them, unimpeded by English transliterations.

Pending the appearance of such an ideal grammar, I have printed here a few of the most useful nouns and verbs, limiting myself as far as possible to the indispensable elements, which every student must learn by heart; and the student who commits to memory the following thirty pages will probably have little difficulty in understanding all the forms he is likely to come across in the first two years of his Sanskrit studies, after which he will probably turn to one of the larger grammars for fuller information.

I have omitted the rules of phonetic assimilation, behind which, as by a formidable outwork, the larger grammars are entrenched. They are best learned by practice—in the actual course of reading—and not by rule beforehand. I have further omitted the accent, and also the rules for variations of declension and conjugation, which can only be properly understood after the actual forms have been learnt by heart; in fact, I have excluded everything which might impede a beginner in the elementary study of a beautiful language, the difficulties of which have been greatly exaggerated.

My thanks are due to Dr. Fitzedward Hall for valuable suggestions.

C. J.

# NOUNS.

# VOWEL STEMS.

## Masculine and Neuter Stems in 'a.'

EXAMPLES: **deva** (masculine), *god*; **jala** (neuter), *water*.

*Singular.*

| | MASCULINE. | | NEUTER. |
|---|---|---|---|
| *Nominative.* | devas | (subject) | jalam |
| *Accusative.* | devam | (direct object) | jalam |
| *Instrumental.* | devena, | *with, by* | jalena |
| *Dative.* | devâya, | *to, for* | jalâya |
| *Ablative.* | devât, | *from, than* | jalât |
| *Genitive.* | devasya, | *of* | jalasya |
| *Locative.* | deve, | *in, at* | jale |
| *Vocative.* | deva, | *O* —— | jala |

*Dual.*

| | | | |
|---|---|---|---|
| *Nominative.* | devâu, | *two* (subject) | jale |
| *Accusative.* | devâu, | *two* (object) | jale |
| *Instrumental.* | devâbhyâm, | *with, by, two* | jalâbhyâm |
| *Dative.* | devâbhyâm, | *to, for, two* | jalâbhyâm |
| *Ablative.* | devâbhyâm, | *from, than, two* | jalâbhyâm |
| *Genitive.* | devayos, | *of two* | jalayos |
| *Locative.* | devayos, | *in, at, two* | jalayos |
| *Vocative.* | devâu, | *O two* —— | jale |

*Plural.*

| | | | |
|---|---|---|---|
| *Nominative.* | devâs | (subject) | jalâni |
| *Accusative.* | devân | (direct object) | jalâni |
| *Instrumental.* | devâis, | *with, by* | jalâis |
| *Dative.* | devebhyas, | *to, for* | jalebhyas |
| *Ablative.* | devebhyas, | *from, than* | jalebhyas |
| *Genitive.* | devânâm, | *of* | jalânâm |
| *Locative.* | deveṣhu, | *in, at* | jaleṣhu |
| *Vocative.* | devâs, | *O* —— | jalâni |

Note Masculine *D.* Dual and *D.* Plural; Neuter, *V.* Singular and *N.* Dual. Decline thus—

| | MASCULINES. | NEUTERS. |
|---|---|---|
| *Nom.* | **Kâmas,** ***Cupid*** | **vanam,** ***wood*** |
| | **hastas,** ***hand*** | **kulam,** ***family*** |
| | **kâkas,** ***crow*** | **dhanam,** ***wealth*** |
| | **mânavas,** ***man*** | **annam,** ***food*** |
| | **analas,** ***fire*** | **puṣhpam,** ***flower*** |
| | **pakṣhas,** ***wing*** | **satyam,** ***truth*** |

## Masculine and Feminine Stems in 'i.'

EXAMPLES: **agni** (masculine), *fire;* **mati** (feminine). *thought.*

*Singular.*

| | MASCULINE. | FEMININE. |
|---|---|---|
| *N.* | agnis | matis |
| *Ac.* | agnim | matim |
| *I.* | agninâ | matyâ |
| *D.* | agnaye | mataye |
| *Ab.* | agnes | mates |
| *G.* | agnes | mates |
| *L.* | agnâu | matâu |
| *V.* | agne | mate |

*Dual.*

| | | |
|---|---|---|
| *N. Ac. V.* | agnî | matî |
| *I. D. Ab.* | agnibhyâm | matibhyâm |
| *G. L.* | agnyos | matyos |

*Plural.*

| | | |
|---|---|---|
| *N.* | agnayas | matayas |
| *Ac.* | agnîn | matîs |
| *I.* | agnibhis | matibhis |
| *D.* | agnibhyas | matibhyas |
| *Ab.* | agnibhyas | matibhyas |
| *G.* | agnînâm | matînâm |
| *L.* | agnishu | matishu |
| *V.* | agnayas | matayas |

Note long *î* in Dual *N.*, *Ac.*, *V.*, and Plural *Ac.*, *G.*, of both genders. Compare *I.* Singular and *Ac.* Plural of Masculine and Feminine. Decline thus—

| | MASCULINES. | FEMININES. |
|---|---|---|
| *Stem.* | kavi, *poet* | ruchi, *ray* |
| | nidhi, *treasure* | gati, *gait* |
| | ravi, *sun* | siddhi, *success* |
| | adhipati, *lord* | nîti, *policy* |
| | ali, *bee* | dyuti, *brightness* |
| | sandhi, *peace* | vipatti, *adversity* |

## Masculine and Feminine Stems in 'u.'

EXAMPLES: **ketu** (masculine), *flag*; **dhenu** (feminine), *cow*.

*Singular.*

| | MASCULINE. | FEMININE. |
|---|---|---|
| *N.* | ketus | dhenus |
| *Ac.* | ketum | dhenum |
| *I.* | ketunâ | dhenvâ |
| *D.* | ketave | dhenave |
| *Ab.* | ketos | dhenos |
| *G.* | ketos | dhenos |
| *L.* | ketâu | dhenâu |
| *V.* | keto | dheno |

*Dual.*

| | | |
|---|---|---|
| *N. Ac. V.* | ketû | dhenû |
| *I. D. Ab.* | ketubhyâm | dhenubhyâm |
| *G. L.* | ketvos | dhenvos |

*Plural.*

| | | |
|---|---|---|
| *N.* | ketavas | dhenavas |
| *Ac.* | ketûn | dhenûs |
| *I.* | ketubhis | dhenubhis |
| *D.* | ketubhyas | dhenubhyas |
| *Ab.* | ketubhyas | dhenubhyas |
| *G.* | ketûnâm | dhenûnâm |
| *L.* | ketuṣhu | dhenuṣhu |
| *V.* | ketavas | dhenavas |

Note long *û* in Dual *N.*, *Ac.*, *V.*, and Plural *Ac.*, *G.*, of both genders. Compare Masculine *I.*, Singular, and *Ac.* Plural with the Feminine. Decline thus—

| | MASCULINES. | FEMININES. |
|---|---|---|
| *Stem.* | vibhu, *master* | chanchu, *beak* |
| | bhânu, *sun* | jambu, *rose-apple* |
| | Manu, *Manu* | tanu, *form* |
| | indu, *moon* | Danu, *Danu* |
| | manyu, *distress* | pṛthu, *opium* |
| | bahu, *much* (masc.) | kâku, *muttering* |

Feminine nouns of this declension are rare.

## Masculine and Feminine Stems in 'ṛ.'

EXAMPLES: **dâtṛ** (masculine), *giver*; **svasṛ** (feminine), *sister*.

*Singular.*

| | MASCULINE. | FEMININE. |
|---|---|---|
| *N.* | dâtâ | svasâ |
| *Ac.* | dâtâram | svasâram |
| *I.* | dâtrâ | svasrâ |
| *D.* | dâtre | svasre |
| *Ab.* | dâtur | svasur |
| *G.* | dâtur | svasur |
| *L.* | dâtari | svasari |
| *V.* | dâtar | svasar |

*Dual.*

| | | |
|---|---|---|
| *N. Ac. V.* | dâtârâu | svasârâu |
| *I. D. Ab.* | dâtṛbhyâm | svasṛbhyâm |
| *G. L.* | dâtros | svasros |

*Plural.*

| | | |
|---|---|---|
| *N.* | dâtâras | svasâras |
| *Ac.* | dâtṝn | svasṝs |
| *I.* | dâtṛbhis | svasṛbhis |
| *D.* | dâtṛbhyas | svasṛbhyas |
| *Ab.* | dâtṛbhyas | svasṛbhyas |
| *G.* | dâtṝṇâm | svasṝṇâm |
| *L.* | dâtṛshu | svasṛshu |
| *V.* | dâtâras | svasâras |

Note long *ṝ* in Plural *Ac. G.* of both genders.

Compare *Ac.* Plural, Masculine, with *Ac.* Plural, Feminine.

Decline like dâtṛ, kartṛ (*a doer*), hotṛ (*a sacrificer*), and, in general, nouns of agency; and also naptṛ (*grandson*). Other masculine nouns of relationship take *ar*, instead of *âr*, in *Ac.* Singular, *N. Ac. V.* Dual, *N. V.* Plural.

Thus pitṛ (*father*) takes pitaram, pitarâu, pitaras. In the same cases, feminine nouns of relationship take *ar*, instead of *âr*, with the exception of svasṛ (*sister*).

Thus mâtṛ (*mother*) takes mâtaram, matarâu, mâtaras.

Subject to these exceptions, masculine and feminine stems in *ṛ* follow the examples given.

## Feminine Stems in 'â, î, û.'

EXAMPLES: **bâlâ,** *girl;* **devî,** *goddess;* **vadhû,** *woman.*

*Singular.*

| | | | |
|---|---|---|---|
| *N.* | bâlâ | devî | vadhûs |
| *Ac.* | bâlâm | devîm | vadhûm |
| *I.* | bâlayâ | devyâ | vadhvâ |
| *D.* | bâlâyâi | devyâi | vadhvâi |
| *Ab.* | bâlâyâs | devyâs | vadhvâs |
| *G.* | bâlâyâs | devyâs | vadhvâs |
| *L.* | bâlâyâm | devyâm | vadhvâm |
| *V.* | bâle | devi | vadhu |

*Dual.*

| | | | |
|---|---|---|---|
| *N. Ac. V.* | bâle | devyâu | vadhvâu |
| *I. D. Ab.* | bâlâbhyâm | devîbhyâm | vadhûbhyâm |
| *G. L.* | bâlayos | devyos | vadhvos |

*Plural.*

| | | | |
|---|---|---|---|
| *N.* | bâlâs | devyas | vadhvas |
| *Ac.* | bâlâs | devîs | vadhûs |
| *I.* | bâlâbhis | devîbhis | vadhûbhis |
| *D.* | bâlâbhyas | devîbhyas | vadhûbhyas |
| *Ab.* | bâlâbhyas | devîbhyas | vadhûbhyas |
| *G.* | bâlânâm | devînâm | vadhûnâm |
| *L.* | bâlâsu | devîṣhu | vadhûṣhu |
| *V.* | bâlâs | devyas | vadhvas |

Note the terminations of *N. Ac. V.* Dual and *N. V.* Plural. Stems in *â* never take final *s* in Nominative Singular; while a few stems in *î* and all stems in *û* take it. Stems in *û* are rare.

Decline thus—

| | | |
|---|---|---|
| senâ, *army* | nadî, *river* | chamû, *army* |
| kanyâ, *girl* | mahî, *earth* | ratû, *heavenly Ganges* |
| mâyâ, *glamour* | rajanî, *night* | âjû, *free labour* |

# CONSONANT STEMS.

## Normal Consonant Stem.

EXAMPLE: **harit,** *green.*

*Singular.*

| | MASCULINE AND FEMININE. | NEUTER. |
|---|---|---|
| *N.* | harit | harit |
| *Ac.* | haritam | harit |
| *I.* | haritâ | haritâ |
| *D.* | harite | harite |
| *Ab.* | haritas | haritas |
| *G.* | haritas | haritas |
| *L.* | hariti | hariti |
| *V.* | harit | harit |

*Dual.*

| | | |
|---|---|---|
| *N. Ac. V.* | haritâu | haritî |
| *I. D. Ab.* | haridbhyâm | haridbhyâm |
| *G. L.* | haritos | haritos |

*Plural.*

| | | |
|---|---|---|
| *N.* | haritas | harinti |
| *Ac.* | haritas | harinti |
| *I.* | haridbhis | haridbhis |
| *D.* | haridbhyas | haridbhyas |
| *Ab.* | haridbhyas | haridbhyas |
| *G.* | haritâm | haritâm |
| *L.* | haritsu | haritsu |
| *V.* | haritas | harinti |

Note the assimilation of the stem with terminations beginning with consonants. The result of these assimilations varies with the final consonant of the stem, and is best learned by practice.

Note the nasalisation of the Neuter Plural *N. Ac. V.*

## Stems in 'in.'

EXAMPLE: **dhanin**, *wealthy*.

*Singular.*

| | MASCULINE. | NEUTER. |
|---|---|---|
| *N.* | dhanî | dhani |
| *Ac.* | dhaninam | dhani |
| *I.* | dhaninâ | dhaninâ |
| *D.* | dhanine | dhanine |
| *Ab.* | dhaninas | dhaninas |
| *G.* | dhaninas | dhaninas |
| *L.* | dhanini | dhanini |
| *V.* | dhanin | dhanin, dhani |

*Dual.*

| | | |
|---|---|---|
| *N. Ac. V.* | dhaninâu | dhaninî |
| *I. D. Ab.* | dhanibhyâm | dhanibhyâm |
| *G. L.* | dhaninos | dhaninos |

*Plural.*

| | | |
|---|---|---|
| *N.* | dhaninas | dhanîni |
| *Ac.* | dhaninas | dhanîni |
| *I.* | dhanibhis | dhanibhis |
| *D.* | dhanibhyas | dhanibhyas |
| *Ab.* | dhanibhyas | dhanibhyas |
| *G.* | dhaninâm | dhaninâm |
| *L.* | dhanishu | dhanishu |
| *V.* | dhaninas | dhanîni |

Note that the stem loses the *n* before consonant terminations.

Note the Neuter *V.* Singular.

Compare Neuter Nominatives, Dual and Plural.

These stems are possessive derivative adjectives in *in*, *vin*, or *min*; the two latter are rare.

Feminines of this class are declined like devî (*e.g.*, dhaninî).

Neuter vowel stems in *i*, *u*, *ṛ*, follow a declension closely analogous to dhani (neuter).

## Stems in 'an.'

EXAMPLES: **râjan** (masculine), *king;* **âtman** (masculine), *self;* **nâman** (neuter), *name.*

*Singular.*

| | MASCULINE. | MASCULINE. | NEUTER. |
|---|---|---|---|
| *N.* | râjâ | âtmâ | nâma |
| *Ac.* | râjânam | âtmânam | nâma |
| *I.* | râjnâ | âtmanâ | nâmnâ |
| *D.* | râjne | âtmane | nâmne |
| *Ab.* | râjnas | âtmanas | nâmnas |
| *G.* | râjnas | âtmanas | nâmnas |
| *L.* | râjni, rajani | âtmani | nâmni, nâmani |
| *V.* | râjan | âtman | nâman, nâma |

*Dual.*

| | | | |
|---|---|---|---|
| *N. Ac. V.* | râjânâu | âtmânâu | nâmnî, nâmanî |
| *I. D. Ab.* | râjabhyâm | âtmabhyâm | nâmabhyâm |
| *G. L.* | râjnos | âtmanos | nâmnos |

*Plural.*

| | | | |
|---|---|---|---|
| *N.* | râjânas | âtmânas | nâmâni |
| *Ac.* | râjnas | âtmanas | nâmâni |
| *I.* | râjabhis | atmabhis | nâmabhis |
| *D.* | râjabhyas | âtmabhyas | nâmabhyas |
| *Ab.* | râjabhyas | âtmabhyas | nâmabhyas |
| *G.* | râjnâm | âtmanâm | nâmnâm |
| *L.* | râjasu | âtmasu | nâmasu |
| *V.* | râjânas | âtmânas | nâmâni |

Note that the stem loses the *n* before consonant terminations.

Note the strong stem (râjân, âtmân) in the *N. Ac.* Singular [râjâ(ns), âtmâ(ns)], *N. Ac. V.* Dual, and *N. V.* Plural of the Masculine.

Note the strong stem (nâmân) in the Neuter *N. Ac. V.* Plural.

Note the contracted stems (râjn, nâmn).

No Feminines follow this declension.

## Stems in 'as.'

EXAMPLES: **sumanas** (masculine and feminine), *well-minded;* **manas** (neuter), *mind.*

*Singular.*

| | MASCULINE AND FEMININE. | NEUTER. |
|---|---|---|
| *N.* | sumanâs | manas |
| *Ac.* | sumanasam | manas |
| *I.* | sumanasâ | manasâ |
| *D.* | sumanase | manase |
| *Ab.* | sumanasas | manasas |
| *G.* | sumanasas | manasas |
| *L.* | sumanasi | manasi |
| *V.* | sumanas | manas |

*Dual.*

| | | |
|---|---|---|
| *N. Ac. V.* | sumanasâu | manasî |
| *I. D. Ab.* | sumanobhyâm | manobhyâm |
| *G. L.* | sumanasos | manasos |

*Plural.*

| | | |
|---|---|---|
| *N.* | sumanasas | manâṅsi |
| *Ac.* | sumanasas | manâṅsi |
| *I.* | sumanobhis | manobhis |
| *D.* | sumanobhyas | manobhyas |
| *Ab.* | sumanobhyas | manobhyas |
| *G.* | sumanasâm | manasâm |
| *L.* | sumanaḥsu | manaḥsu |
| *V.* | sumanasas | manâṅsi |

**Note the assimilation of the stem (*o* for *as*) with terminations beginning with sonant consonants. An analogous change (*ah* for *as*) *may* take place in the *L.* Plural.**

**Note the nasalisation of the Neuter Plural *N. Ac. V.* (*âṅsi* is pronounced like *anci* in the French *ancien*).**

## Stems in 'ant' (at).

EXAMPLES: **mahat**, *great;* **agnimat**, *fiery;* **bhavat**, *being.*

MASCULINE.

*Singular.*

| | | | |
|---|---|---|---|
| *N.* | mahân | agnimân | bhavan |
| *Ac.* | mahântam | agnimantam | bhavantam |
| *I.* | mahatâ | agnimatâ | bhavatâ |
| *D.* | mahate | agnimate | bhavate |
| *Ab.* | mahatas | agnimatas | bhavatas |
| *G.* | mahatas | agnimatas | bhavatas |
| *L.* | mahati | agnimati | bhavati |
| *V.* | mahan | agniman | bhavan |

*Dual.*

| | | | |
|---|---|---|---|
| *N. Ac. V.* | mahântâu | agnimantâu | bhavantâu |
| *I. D. A.* | mahadbhyâm | agnimadbhyâm | bhavadbhyâm |
| *G. L.* | mahatos | agnimatos | bhavatos |

*Plural.*

| | | | |
|---|---|---|---|
| *N.* | mahântas | agnimantas | bhavantas |
| *Ac.* | mahatas | agnimatas | bhavatas |
| *I.* | mahadbhis | agnimadbhis | bhavadbhis |
| *D.* | mahadbhyas | agnimadbhyas | bhavadbhyas |
| *Ab.* | mahadbhyas | agnimadbhyas | bhavadbhyas |
| *G.* | mahatâm | agnimatâm | bhavatâm |
| *L.* | mahatsu | agnimatsu | bhavatsu |
| *V.* | mahântas | agnimantas | bhavantas |

NEUTER.

*Singular.*

| | | | |
|---|---|---|---|
| *N. Ac. V.* | mahat | agnimat | bhavat |

*Dual.*

| | | | |
|---|---|---|---|
| *N. Ac. V.* | mahatî | agnimatî | bhavantî |

*Plural.*

| | | | |
|---|---|---|---|
| *N. Ac. V.* | mahânti | agnimanti | bhavanti |

The oblique cases, Neuter, are the same as the Masculine. Note *N.*, *V.*, *Ac.* all through, especially Neuter Dual of bhavat. The Feminines mahatî, agnimatî, bhavantî (which are the same in form as the Neuter Dual) are declined like devî.

## Stems in 'yâṅs' (yas) and 'vâṅs' (uṣh).

EXAMPLES: **shreyâṅs,** *better,* and **vidvâṅs,** *knowing.*

MASCULINE.

*Singular.*

| | | |
|---|---|---|
| *N.* | shreyân | vidvân |
| *Ac.* | shreyâṅsam | vidvâṅsam |
| *I.* | shreyasâ | viduṣhâ |
| *D.* | shreyase | viduṣhe |
| *Ab.* | shreyasas | viduṣhas |
| *G.* | shreyasas | viduṣhas |
| *L.* | shreyasi | viduṣhi |
| *V.* | shreyan | vidvan |

*Dual.*

| | | |
|---|---|---|
| *N. Ac. V.* | shreyâṅsâu | vidvâṅsâu |
| *I. D. Ab.* | shreyobhyâm | vidvadbhyâm |
| *G. L.* | shreyasos | viduṣhos |

*Plural.*

| | | |
|---|---|---|
| *N.* | shreyâṅsas | vidvâṅsas |
| *Ac.* | shreyasas | viduṣhas |
| *I.* | shreyobhis | vidvadbhis |
| *D.* | shreyobhyas | vidvadbhyas |
| *Ab.* | shreyobhyas | vidvadbhyas |
| *G.* | shreyasâm | viduṣhâm |
| *L.* | shreyaḥsu | vidvatsu |
| *V.* | shreyâṅsas | vidvâṅsas |

NEUTER.

*Singular.*

| | | |
|---|---|---|
| *N. Ac. V.* | shreyas | vidvat |

*Dual.*

| | | |
|---|---|---|
| *N. Ac. V.* | shreyasî | viduṣhî |

*Plural.*

| | | |
|---|---|---|
| *N. Ac. V.* | shreyâṅsi | vidvâṅsi |

The other cases of the Neuter are the same as the Masculine.

The Feminines shreyasî, viduṣhî (*cf.* Neuter Dual), are declined like devî.

Stems in *yâṅs* or *îyâṅs* are Comparatives.

Stems in *vâṅs* are Perfect Participles Active.

(The *âṅs* is pronounced like *anc* in French *ancien.*)

# PRONOUNS AND PRONOMINALS.

## First and Second Person.

| **Base** (in composition), *mad* and *asmad.* | | | **Base** (in composition), *tvad* and *yushmad.* | |
|---|---|---|---|---|
| | | *Singular.* | | |
| *N.* | aham, *I* | | tvam, *thou* | |
| *Ac.* | mâm | mâ | tvâm | tvâ |
| *I.* | mayâ | | tvayâ | |
| *D.* | mahyam | me | tubhyam | te |
| *Ab.* | mat | | tvat | |
| *G.* | mama | me | tava | te |
| *L.* | mayi | | tvayi | |
| | | *Dual.* | | |
| *N.* | âvâm, *we two* | | yuvâm, *you two* | |
| *Ac.* | âvâm | nâu | yuvâm | vâm |
| *I.* | âvâbhyâm | | yuvâbhyâm | |
| *D.* | âvâbhyâm | nâu | yuvâbhyâm | vâm |
| *Ab.* | âvâbhyâm | | yuvâbhyâm | |
| *G.* | âvayos | nâu | yuvayos | vâm |
| *L.* | âvayos | | yuvayos | |
| | | *Plural.* | | |
| *N.* | vayam, *we* | | yûyam, *you* | |
| *Ac.* | asmân | nas | yushmân | vas |
| *I.* | asmâbhis | | yushmâbhis | |
| *D.* | asmabhyam | nas | yushmabhyam | vas |
| *Ab.* | asmat | | yushmat | |
| *G.* | asmâkam | nas | yushmâkam | vas |
| *L.* | asmâsu | | yushmâsu | |

Note the alternative forms for alternate cases.

These alternative forms cannot be used at the beginning of a sentence.

These pronouns have no distinction of gender. They are very irregular, and should be committed to memory before any attempt is made to explain their forms.

# DEMONSTRATIVES, INTERROGATIVES, AND RELATIVES.

## MASCULINE.

*Singular.*

| | *this.* | *he.* | *this (near).* | *who?* | *who.* |
|---|---|---|---|---|---|
| *N.* | [ayam] | [sas] | [eshas] | kas | yas |
| *Ac.* | [imam] | tam | etam | kam | yam |
| *I.* | [anena] | tena | etena | kena | yena |
| *D.* | asmâi | tasmâi | etasmâi | kasmâi | yasmâi |
| *Ab.* | asmât | tasmât | etasmât | kasmât | yasmât |
| *G.* | asya | tasya | etasya | kasya | yasya |
| *L.* | asmin | tasmin | etasmin | kasmin | yasmin |

*Dual.*

| | | | | | |
|---|---|---|---|---|---|
| *N. Ac.* | [imâu] | tâu | etâu | kâu | yâu |
| *I. D. Ab.* | âbhyâm | tâbhyâm | etâbhyâm | kâbhyâm | yâbhyâm |
| *G. L.* | [anayos] | tayos | etayos | kayos | yayos |

*Plural.*

| | | | | | |
|---|---|---|---|---|---|
| *N.* | [ime] | te | ete | ke | ye |
| *Ac.* | [imân] | tân | etân | kân | yân |
| *I.* | ebhis | tâis | etâis | kâis | yâis |
| *D.* | ebhyas | tebhyas | etebhyas | kebhyas | yebhyas |
| *Ab.* | ebhyas | tebhyas | etebhyas | kebhyas | yebhyas |
| *G.* | eṣhâm | teṣhâm | eteṣhâm | keṣhâm | yeṣhâm |
| *L.* | eṣhu | teṣhu | eteṣhu | keṣhu | yeṣhu |

## NEUTER.

*Singular.*

| | | | | | |
|---|---|---|---|---|---|
| *N. Ac.* | [idam] | tat | etat | kim | yat |

*Dual.*

| | | | | | |
|---|---|---|---|---|---|
| *N. Ac.* | [ime] | te | ete | ke | ye |

*Plural.*

| | | | | | |
|---|---|---|---|---|---|
| *N. Ac.* | [imâni] | tâni | etâni | kâni | yâni |

The forms in brackets are taken from other roots, to supply defective cases. Note the Instrumental Plural.

Like *kas* are declined the Pronominals; for example, ekas, *one;* sarvas, *each, every;* anyas, *other;* svas, *own;* uttaras, *north;* dakṣhiṇas, *south;* pûrvas, *east;* adharas, *west;* except that they make the Neuter Singular *N. Ac.* thus: ekam, sarvam, anyat, svam, uttaram, dakṣhiṇam, pûrvam, adharam. They make Masc. Sing. *V.*, eka, sarva, &c.

## Demonstratives, Interrogatives, and Relatives, —*continued.*

### FEMININE.

*Singular.*

| | | | | | |
|---|---|---|---|---|---|
| *N.* | [iyam] | [sâ] *she* | [eshâ] | kâ | yâ |
| *Ac.* | [imâm] | tâm | etâm | kâm | yâm |
| *I.* | [anayâ] | tayâ | etayâ | kayâ | yayâ |
| *D.* | asyâi | tasyâi | etasyâi | kasyâi | yasyâi |
| *Ab.* | asyâs | tasyâs | etasyâs | kasyâs | yasyâs |
| *G.* | asyâs | tasyâs | etasyâs | kasyâs | yasyâs |
| *L.* | asyâm | tasyâm | etasyâm | kasyâm | yasyâm |

*Dual.*

| | | | | | |
|---|---|---|---|---|---|
| *N. Ac.* | [ime] | te | ete | ke | ye |
| *I. D. Ab.* | âbhyâm | tâbhyâm | etâbhyâm | kâbhyâm | yâbhyâm |
| *G. L.* | [anayos] | tayos | etayos | kayos | yayos |

*Plural.*

| | | | | | |
|---|---|---|---|---|---|
| *N.* | [imâs] | tâs | etâs | kâs | yâs |
| *Ac.* | [imâs] | tâs | etâs | kâs | yâs |
| *I.* | âbhis | tâbhis | etâbhis | kâbhis | yâbhis |
| *D.* | âbhyas | tâbhyas | etâbhyas | kâbhyas | yâbhyas |
| *Ab.* | âbhyas | tâbhyas | etâbhyas | kâbhyas | yâbhyas |
| *G.* | âsâm | tâsâm | etâsâm | kâsâm | yâsam |
| *L.* | âsu | tâsu | etâsu | kâsu | yâsu |

The forms in brackets are taken from other roots, to supply defective cases.

## Adverbs from the same Roots.

| | Demonstrative. | | Interrogative. | Relative. |
|---|---|---|---|---|
| | (Near.) | (Remote.) | | |
| Time . . . | idânîm .. *now* | tadâ, *then* | kadâ, *when?* | yadâ, *when* |
| Mode . . | .. atha, *so* | tathâ, *thus* | .. | yathâ, *as* |
| Mode . . | itham .. *thus* | .. | katham, *how?* | .. |
| Sequence . | itas atas, *hence* | tatas, *thence* | kutas, *whence?* | yatas, *whence* |
| Place. . . | .. atra, *here* | tatra, *there* | kutra, *where?* | yatra, *where* |
| Comparison | .. .. .. | tâvat, *so far* | .. | yâvat, *as far* |

Similar adverbs are formed from the pronominals: ekadâ, *once*; anyatra, *elsewhere*; sarvadâ, *always*.

# VERBS.

## Bhû.

| *Gerund.* | *Infinitive.* | *Compound Gerund.* |
|---|---|---|
| **bhûtvâ,** | **bhavitum,** | **anu-bhûya,** |
| *having been.* | *to be.* | *having perceived.* |

| | Active. | Middle. | Passive. |
|---|---|---|---|
| | | *Present Participle.* | |
| | bhavan, -antî, -at. | bhavamânas, -â, -am. | bhûyamânas, -a, -am. |
| | | *Indicative.* | |
| *Sing.* | bhavâmi | bhave | bhûye |
| | bhavasi | bhavase | bhûyase |
| | bhavati | bhavate | bhûyate |
| *Dual.* | bhavâvas | bhavâvahe | bhûyâvahe |
| | bhavathas | bhavethe | bhûyethe |
| | bhavatas | bhavete | bhûyete |
| *Plural.* | bhavâmas | bhavâmahe | bhûyâmahe |
| | bhavatha | bhavadhve | bhûyadhve |
| | bhavanti | bhavante | bhûyante |
| | | *Optative.* | |
| *Sing.* | bhaveyam | bhaveya | bhûyeya |
| | bhaves | bhavethâs | bhûyethâs |
| | bhavet | bhaveta | bhûyeta |
| *Dual.* | bhaveva | bhavevahi | bhûyevahi |
| | bhavetam | bhaveyâthâm | bhûyeyâthâm |
| | bhavetâm | bhaveyâtâm | bhûyeyâtâm |
| *Plural.* | bhevema | bhavemahi | bhûyemahi |
| | bhaveta | bhavedhvam | bhûyedhvam |
| | bhaveyus | bhaveran | bhûyeran |
| | | *Imperative.* | |
| *Sing.* | bhavâni | bhavâi | bhûyâi |
| | bhava | bhavasva | bhûyasva |
| | bhavatu | bhavatâm | bhûyatâm |
| *Dual.* | bhavâva | bhavâvahâi | bhûyâvahâi |
| | bhavatam | bhavethâm | bhûyethâm |
| | bhavatâm | bhavetâm | bhûyetâm |
| *Plural.* | bhavâma | bhavâmahâi | bhûyâmahâi |
| | bhavata | bhavadhvam | bhûyadhvam |
| | bhavantu | bhavantâm | bhûyantâm |

## Bhû—*continued.*

| | Active. | Middle. | Passive. |
|---|---|---|---|
| | | *Imperfect.* | |
| *Sing.* | abhavam | abhave | abhûye |
| | abhavas | abhavathâs | abhûyathâs |
| | abhavat | abhavata | abhûyata |
| *Dual.* | abhavâva | abhavâvahi | abhûyâvahi |
| | abhavatam | abhavethâm | abhûyethâm |
| | abhavatâm | abhavetâm | abhûyetâm |
| *Plural.* | abhavâma | abhavâmahi | abhûyâmahi |
| | abhavata | abhavadhvam | abhûyadhvam |
| | abhavan | abhavanta | abhûyanta |
| | | *Future Indicative.* | |
| *Sing.* | bhavishyâmi | bhavishye | bhâvishye |
| | bhavishyasi | bhavishyase | bhâvishyase |
| | bhavishyati | bhavishyate | bhâvishyate |
| *Dual.* | bhavishyâvas | bhavishyâvahe | bhâvishyâvahe |
| | bhavishyathas | bhavishyethe | bhâvishyethe |
| | bhavishyatas | bhavishyete | bhâvishyete |
| *Plural.* | bhavishyâmas | bhavishyâmahe | bhâvishyâmahe |
| | bhavishyatha | bhavishyadhve | bhâvishyadhve |
| | bhavishyanti | bhavishyante | bhâvishyante |
| | | *Participle.* | |
| | bhavishyan, -antî, -at. | bhavishyamâṇas, -â, -am. | bhavishyamâṇas, -â, -am. |
| | | *Perfect Indicative.* | |
| *Sing.* | babhûva | babhûve | babhûve |
| | babhûvitha | babhûvishe | babhûvishe |
| | babhûva | babhûve | babhûve |
| *Dual.* | babhûviva | babhûvivahe | babhûvivahe |
| | babhûvathus | babhûvâthe | babhûvâthe |
| | babhûvatus | babhûvâte | babhûvâte |
| *Plural.* | babhûvima | babhûvimahe | babhûvimahe |
| | babhûva | babhûvidhve | babhûvidhve |
| | babhûvus | babhûvire | babhûvire |
| | | *Participle.* | |
| | babhûvân, -vushî, -vat. | babhûvânas, -â, -am. | bhûtas, -â, -am. |

## Su.

| *Gerund.* | *Infinitive.* | *Compound Gerund.* |
|---|---|---|
| **sutvâ,** | **sotum,** | **abhi-sûya,** |
| *having distilled.* | *to distil.* | *having sprinkled.* |

| | Active. | Middle. | Passive. |
|---|---|---|---|
| | | *Present Participle.* | |
| | sunvan, | sunvânas, | sûyamânas, |
| | -vatî, -vat | -â, -am | -â, -am |
| | | *Indicative.* | |
| *Sing.* | sunomi | sunve | sûye |
| | sunoṣhi | sunuṣhe | sûyase |
| | sunoti | sunute | sûyate |
| *Dual.* | sunuvas | sunuvahe | sûyâvahẹ |
| | sunuthas | sunvâthe | sûyethe |
| | sunutas | sunvâte | sûyete |
| *Plural.* | sunumas | sunumahe | sûyâmahe |
| | sunutha | sunudhve | sûyadhve |
| | sunvanti | sunvate | sûyante |
| | | *Optative.* | |
| *Sing.* | sunuyâm | sunvîya | sûyeya |
| | sunuyâs | sunvîthâs | sûyethâs |
| | sunuyât | sunvîta | sûyeta |
| *Dual.* | sunuyâva | sunvîvahi | sûyevahi |
| | sunuyâtam | sunvîyâthâm | sûyeyâthâm |
| | sunuyâtâm | sunvîyâtâm | sûyeyâtâm |
| *Plural.* | sunuyâma | sunvîmahi | sûyemahi |
| | sunuyâta | sunvîdhvam | sûyedhvam |
| | sunuyus | sunvîran | sûyeran |
| | | *Imperative.* | |
| *Sing.* | sunavâni | sunavâi | sûyâi |
| | sunu | sunuṣhva | sûyasva |
| | sunotu | sunutâm | sûyatâm |
| *Dual.* | sunavâva | sunavâvahâi | sûyâvahâi |
| | sunutam | sunvâthâm | sûyethâm |
| | sunutâm | sunvâtâm | sûyetâm |
| *Plural.* | sunavâma | sunavâmahâi | sûyâmahâi |
| | sunuta | sunudhvam | sûyadhvam |
| | sunvantu | sunvatâm | sûyantâm |

## Su—*continued.*

| | ACTIVE. | MIDDLE. | PASSIVE. |
|---|---|---|---|
| | | *Imperfect.* | |
| *Sing.* | asunavam | asunvi | asûye |
| | asunos | asunuthâs | asûyathâs |
| | asunot | asunuta | asûyata |
| *Dual.* | asunuva | asunuvahi | asûyâvahi |
| | asunutam | asunvâthâm | asûyethâm |
| | asunutâm | asunvâtâm | asûyetâm |
| *Plural.* | asunuma | asunumahi | asûyâmahi |
| | asunuta | asunudhvam | asûyadhvam |
| | asunvan | asunvata | asûyanta |
| | | *Future Indicative.* | |
| *Sing.* | soṣhyâmi | soṣhye | soṣhye |
| | soṣhyasi | soṣhyase | soṣhyase |
| | soṣhyati | soṣhyate | soṣhyate |
| *Dual.* | soṣhyâvas | soṣhyâvahe | soṣhyâvahe |
| | soṣhyathas | soṣhyethe | soṣhyethe |
| | soṣhyatas | soṣhyete | soṣhyete |
| *Plural.* | soṣhyâmas | soṣhyâmahe | soṣhyâmahe |
| | soṣhyatha | soṣhyadhve | soṣhyadhve |
| | soṣhyanti | soṣhyante | soṣhyante |
| | | *Participle.* | |
| | soṣhyan, -antî, -at | soṣhyamâṇas, -â, -am | soṣhyamâṇas, -â, -am |
| | | *Perfect Indicative.* | |
| *Sing.* | suṣhâva | suṣhuve | suṣhuve |
| | suṣhotha | suṣhuviṣhe | suṣhuviṣhe |
| | suṣhâva | suṣhuve | suṣhuve |
| *Dual.* | suṣhuviva | suṣhuvivahe | suṣhuvivahe |
| | suṣhuvathus | suṣhuvâthe | suṣhuvâthe |
| | suṣhuvatus | suṣhuvâte | suṣhuvâte |
| *Plural.* | suṣhuvima | suṣhuvimahe | suṣhuvimahe |
| | suṣhuva | suṣhuvidhve | suṣhuvidhve |
| | suṣhuvus | suṣhuvire | suṣhuvire |
| | | *Participle.* | |
| | suṣhuvân, -vuṣhî, -vat | suṣhuvâṇas, -â, -am | sutas, -â, -am |

## Jnâ.

| *Gerund.* | *Infinitive.* | *Compound Gerund.* |
|---|---|---|
| **jnâtvâ,** | **jnâtûm,** | **prati-jnâya,** |
| *having known.* | *to know.* | *having promised.* |

*Present Participle.*

| ACTIVE. | MIDDLE. | PASSIVE. |
|---|---|---|
| jânan, -atî, -at | jânânas, -â, -am | jnâyamânas,-â,-am |

*Indicative.*

| | | | |
|---|---|---|---|
| *Sing.* | jânâmi | jâne | jnâye |
| | jânâsi | jânîṣhe | jnâyase |
| | jânâti | jânîte | jnâyate |
| *Dual.* | jânîvas | jânîvahe | jnâyâvahe |
| | jânîthas | jânâthe | jnâyethe |
| | jânîtas | jânâte | jnâyete |
| *Plural.* | jânîmas | jânîmahe | jnâyâmahe |
| | jânîtha | jânîdhve | jnâyadhve |
| | jânanti | jânate | jnâyante |

*Optative.*

| | | | |
|---|---|---|---|
| *Sing.* | jânîyâm | jânîya | jnâyeya |
| | jânîyâs | jânîthâs | jnâyethâs |
| | jânîyât | jânîta | jnâyeta |
| *Dual.* | jânîyâva | jânîvahi | jnâyevahi |
| | jânîyâtam | jânîyâthâm | jnâyeyâthâm |
| | jânîyâtâm | jânîyâtâm | jnâyeyâtâm |
| *Plural.* | jânîyâma | jânîmahi | jnâyemahi |
| | jânîyâta | jânîdhvam | jnâyedhvam |
| | jânîyus | jânîran | jnâyeran |

*Imperative.*

| | | | |
|---|---|---|---|
| *Sing.* | jânâni | jânâi | jnâyâi |
| | jânîhi | jânîṣhva | jnâyasva |
| | jânâtu | jânîtâm | jnâyatâm |
| *Dual.* | jânâva | jânâvahâi | jnâyâvahâi |
| | jânîtam | jânâthâm | jnâyethâm |
| | jânîtâm | jânâtâm | jnâyetâm |
| *Plural.* | jânâma | jânâmahâi | jnâyâmahâi |
| | jânîta | jânîdhvam | jnâyadhvam |
| | jânantu | jânatâm | jnâyantâm |

Note that the Imperative, Second Person Singular, of gṛhṇâmi is gṛhâṇa.

## Jnâ—*continued.*

| | ACTIVE. | MIDDLE. | PASSIVE. |
|---|---|---|---|
| | | *Imperfect.* | |
| *Sing.* | ajânâm | ajâni | ajnâye |
| | ajânâs | ajânîthâs | ajnâyathâs |
| | ajânât | ajânîta | ajnâyata |
| *Dual.* | ajânîva | ajânîvahi | ajnâyâvahi |
| | ajânîtam | ajânâthâm | ajnâyethâm |
| | ajânîtâm | ajânâtâm | ajnâyetâm |
| *Plural.* | ajânîma | ajânîmahi | ajnâyâmahi |
| | ajânîta | ajânîdhvam | ajnâyadhvam |
| | ajânan | ajânata | ajnâyanta |
| | | *Future Indicative.* | |
| *Sing.* | jnâsyâmi | jnâsye | jnâsye |
| | jnâsyasi | jnâsyase | jnâsyase |
| | jnâsyati | jnâsyate | jnâsyate |
| *Dual.* | jnâsyâvas | jnâsyâvahe | jnâsyâvahe |
| | jnâsyathas | jnâsyethe | jnâsyethe |
| | jnâsyatas | jnâsyete | jnâsyete |
| *Plural.* | jnâsyâmas | jnâsyâmahe | jnâsyâmahe |
| | jnâsyatha | jnâsyadhve | jnâsyadhve |
| | jnâsyanti | jnâsyante | jnâsyante |
| | | *Participle.* | |
| | jnâsyan, -antî, -at | jnâsyamânas, -â, -am | jnâsyamânas, -â, -am |
| | | *Perfect Indicative.* | |
| *Sing.* | jajnâu | jajne | jajne |
| | jajnâtha | jajnishe | jajnishe |
| | jajnâu | jajne | jajne |
| *Dual.* | jajniva | jajnivahe | jajnivahe |
| | jajnathus | jajnâthe | jajnâthe |
| | jajnatus | jajnâte | jajnâte |
| *Plural.* | jajnima | jajnimahe | jajnimahe |
| | jajna | jajnidhve | jajnidhve |
| | jajnus | jajnire | jajnire |
| | | *Participle.* | |
| | jajnivân, -nushî, -nivat | jajnânas, -â, -am | jnâtas, -â, -am |

## As.

*Infinitive.* **astum,** *to be.*

*Participle.* **san, satî, sat,** *being.*

| | *Present Indicative.* | *Optative.* | *Imperative.* |
|---|---|---|---|
| *Sing.* | asmi | syâm | asâni |
| | asi | syâs | edhi |
| | asti | syât | astu |
| *Dual.* | svas | syâva | asâva |
| | sthas | syâtam | stam |
| | stas | syâtâm | stâm |
| *Plural.* | smas | syâma | asâma |
| | stha | syâta | sta |
| | santi | syus | santu |

| | *Imperfect.* | *Perfect Active.* | *Perfect Middle.* |
|---|---|---|---|
| *Sing.* | âsam | âsa | âse |
| | âsîs | âsitha | âsishe |
| | âsît | âsa | âse |
| *Dual.* | âsva | âsiva | âsivahe |
| | âstam | âsathus | âsâthe |
| | âstâm | âsatus | âsâte |
| *Plural.* | âsma | âsima | âsimahe |
| | âsta | âsa | âsidhve |
| | âsan | âsus | âsire |

**brû,** *to speak,* with defective perfect **âha**.

| | *Present Indicative.* | *Imperative.* | *Imperfect.* | *Perfect.* |
|---|---|---|---|---|
| *Sing.* | bravîmi | bravâni | abravam | |
| | bravîshi | brûhi | abravîs | âttha |
| | bravîti | bravîtu | abravît | âha |
| *Dual.* | brûvas | bravâva | abrûva | |
| | brûthas | brûtam | abrûtam | âhathus |
| | brûtas | brûtâm | abrûtâm | âhatus |
| *Plural.* | brûmas | bravâma | abrûma | |
| | brûtha | brûta | abrûta | |
| | bruvanti | bruvantu | abruvan | âhus |

The optative is brûyâm ; brû is defective in the other tenses.

## A HUNDRED USEFUL ROOTS.

âp, *obtain*
âs, *sit*
i, *go*
iṣh, *wish*
îkṣh, *see*
îsh, *rule*
kam, *love*
kâsh, *shine*
kṛ, *do*
kṛt, *cut*
kram, *pace*
kṣham, *bear*
kṣhi, *wane*
khad, *eat*
khyâ, *proclaim*
gam, *go*
gup, *protect*
guh, *hide*
gâi, *sing*
grah, *grasp*
chit, *think*
jan, *produce*
ji, *conquer*
jṝ, *fade*
tan, *tend*
tap, *burn*
tṛp, *delight*
tras, *tremble*
tṝ, *cross*
tvar, *hurry*
dam, *tame*
dah, *burn*
dâ, *give*
dṛsh, *see*
dyut, *shine*
dviṣh, *hate*
dhâ, *place*
nad, *sound*
nam, *bend*
nash, *perish*
nind, *blame*
pat, *fall*
pad, *go*
pashya, *see*
pâ, *drink*
pû, *purify*
pṝ, *fill*
phal, *produce*
bandh, *bind*
budh, *know*
bhî, *fear*
bhṛ, *bear*
bhram, *roam*
manth, *strike*
mâ, *measure*
much, *loosen*
muh, *err*
mṛ, *die*
mnâ, *study*
yaj, *sacrifice*
yam, *restrain*
yâ, *go*
ranj, *tinge*
ram, *sport*
râj, *shine*
vach, *speak*
vad, *speak*
vas, *dwell*
vah, *carry*
vid, *find*
vid, *know*
viṣh, *pervade*
vṛ, *choose*
vṛt, *be*
vṛdh, *grow*
vyath, *fear*
vraj, *go*
shak, *can*
shâs, *command*
shiṣh, *leave*
shî, *lie*
shri, *serve*
shru, *hear*
shvas, *breathe*
sad, *perish*
sanj, *stick*
sâdh, *complete*
sṛj, *abandon*
stu, *praise*
stṝ, *cover*
sthâ, *stand*
spṛsh, *touch*
svap, *sleep*
han, *kill*
hâ, *leave*
hiṅs, *injure*
hu, *sacrifice*
hṛ, *take*
hrî, *shame*
hve, *call*

*Printed by* BALLANTYNE, HANSON & CO., *Edinburgh and London*